D1498336

The Sinking
of the Titanic

Books by Hans Magnus Enzensberger

POEMS FOR PEOPLE WHO DON'T READ POEMS
THE HAVANA INQUIRY
THE CONSCIOUSNESS INDUSTRY
RAIDS AND RECONSTRUCTIONS
MAUSOLEUM
THE SINKING OF THE TITANIC

HANS MAGNUS ENZENSBERGER

The Sinking
of the Titanic

A Poem

Translated by the author

HOUGHTON MIFFLIN COMPANY BOSTON 1980

F56460

© Suhrkamp Verlag Frankfurt am Mein 1978
Translation copyright © 1980 by Hans Magnus Enzensberger

Library of Congress Cataloging in Publication Data

Enzensberger, Hans Magnus.
  The Sinking of the Titanic.
  Translation of Der Untergang der Titanic.
  I. Title.
PT2609.N9U513   831'.914   79–28573
ISBN 0–395–29120–8
ISBN 0–395–29121–6 pbk.

Printed in the United States of America

v 10 9 8 7 6 5 4 3 2 1

Two sections of this work, "Identity Check"
and "Notice of Loss," have appeared in *The Paris Review*.

FOR GASTÓN

CONTENTS

The Sinking of the Titanic

FIRST CANTO

There is someone who listens, who waits,
holds his breath, very close by,
here. He says: This is *my* voice.

Never again, he says,
is it going to be as quiet,
as dry and warm as it is now.

He hears himself
in his gurgling head.
He says: There is no one here

but me. This must be *my* voice.
I wait, I hold my breath,
I listen. The distant rumor

in my ears, antennae
of soft flesh, means nothing.
It is just the beat

of my blood in the veins.
I have been waiting for a long time,
holding my breath.

White noise in the earphones
of my time machine.
Mute cosmic static.

Nobody knocks or cries for help.
No radio signal.
Either this is the end,

I tell myself, or else
we have not yet begun.
Here we are! Now!

A scraping sound. A creaking. A crack.
This is it. An icy fingernail
scratching at the door and stopping short.

Something gives.
An endless length of canvas,
a snow-white strip of linen

being torn, slowly at first
and then more and more briskly
being rent in two with a hissing sound.

This is the beginning.
Listen! Don't you hear it?
Hold fast, for God's sake!

Then there is silence again.
Only a thin tinkle is to be heard
in the cupboards,

a trembling of crystal,
more and more faintly
and dying away.

Do you mean to say
that was all?
Yes. We've had it.

This was the beginning.
The beginning of the end
is always discreet.

It is now 11:40 P.M.
on board. There is a gash
of two hundred yards

underneath the waterline
in the steel-plated hull, slit
by a gigantic knife.

The water is rushing
into the bulkheads.
Thirty yards above sea level

the iceberg, back and silent, passes,
glides by the glittering ship,
and disappears in the dark.

SECOND CANTO

The impact was very slight. The first radiogram:
*0015 hours Mayday CQ Position 41° 46′ North
50° 14′ West.* Marvelous chap, this Marconi!
A ticker inside your head, in the earpiece,
wireless and far, far away, more than half a century!
No sirens, no alarm bells, just a discreet knock
at the cabin door, a subdued cough
in the smoking lounge. While down below
the water is rising fast, on D-deck the steward
is lacing the boots of a groaning old gentleman
in the machine-tool and smelting trade.
Courage, my ladies! Full tilt! That's the way!
The cheers of the athletics coach, Mr MacCawley,
always immaculate in his dapper beige flannel suit,
ring across the paneled gymnasium.
The mechanical camels seesaw in silence.
Nobody knows that the unflagging sportsman
has a weak stomach, that he cannot swim,
that he is yellow. John Jacob Astor, nail file
in hand, rips up a lifesaver in order to show
to his wife (née Connaught) what is inside
(probably cork), while the water is pouring
in torrents into the forehold, swirling mailbags
in icy eddies, and trickling into the pantries.
Wigl wagl wak, my monkey, bleats the band,
dressed in snow-white gala uniforms:
a potpourri from *The Dollar Princess.*
A night at the Metropole! Berlin at its very best!

Those down below are always the first
to understand danger. Hastily they collect
their bundles, babies and ruby-red feather beds.

4

The steerage may not be fluent in English or German,
but it does not need an interpreter to find out
that the First Class is always first served
and that there are never enough milk bottles,
shoes or lifeboats for all of us.

Apocalypse. Umbrian Master, about 1490

He is not as young as he used to be. With a groan
he chooses a sizable canvas. He broods on it.
He wastes his time haggling about his commission
with a mean Carmelite monk from the Abruzzi,
prior, or canon, or whatnot. It is winter now.
His finger joints start cracking like the brushwood
in the fireplace. With a groan he will ground
the canvas, let it dry, ground it once more,
will scrawl his figures, impatiently, ghostlike,
on small cartoons, and set them off with white lead.
He temporizes and idles away a few weeks,
rubbing down his colors. But at long last —
Ash Wednesday has gone by, and Candlemas —
early one morning he dips his brush in burnt umber
and starts painting. This will be a gloomy picture.
How do you go about painting Doom? The conflagrations,
the vanishing islands, the lightning, the walls
and towers and pinnacles crumbling ever so slowly:
nice points of technique, problems of composition.
Destroying the world is a difficult exercise.
Hardest to paint are the sounds — for example
the temple veil being rent asunder, the beasts
roaring, and the thunderclaps. Everything, you see,
is to be rent asunder and torn to pieces,
except the canvas. And there can be no doubt
about the appointed time: by All Souls' Day
the frantic sea in the background must be coated
over and over again with a thousand layers
of transparency, with foamy green lights,
pierced by mastheads, by ships reeling, plunging down,
by wrecks, while outside, in mid-July,
not a dog will stir on the dust-covered square.

The women have left, the servants, the disciples.
In the forlorn town only the Master remains.
He looks tired. Who would have thought that he, of all people,
would look dead tired? Ochre — everything seems ochre now,
shadowless, standing still, transfixed in a kind
of evil eternity, except the picture. It grows
and darkens slowly, absorbing shadows,
steel-blue; livid, dull violet, caput mortuum,
absorbing demons and horsemen and massacres,
until Doom is happily consummated and the artist,
for a brief moment, is, like a child, unmindfully merry,
as if his life had been spared, and in his relief
on this very night he asks his friends to a feast
and treats them to truffles, to grouse and old wine,
with the season's first rainstorm pounding away at the shutters.

THIRD CANTO

I remember Havana, the plaster coming down
from the walls, a foul insistent smell
choking the harbor, the past voluptuously fading,
and scarcity gnawing away, day and night,
at the Ten Year Plan, full of longing,
while I worked at *The Sinking of the Titanic*.
There were no shoes, no toys, no light bulbs,
and there was not a moment of calm, ever,
and the rumors over the crowd
were thick as flies. I remember us thinking:
Tomorrow things will be better, and if not
tomorrow, then the day after. O.K. —
perhaps not much better really,
but different, anyway. Yes, everything
was going to be quite different. -
A marvelous feeling. Oh, I remember it.

I write these words in Berlin, and like Berlin
I smell of old cartridge cases,
of the East, of sulfur, of disinfectant.
It is getting colder again, little by little,
and little by little I'm reading the regulations.
In the distance there is the Wall, unnoticed,
hidden by many movie houses, and behind it
a few desolate movie houses disappear in the distance.
I see lonely foreigners in brand-new shoes
deserting across the snow in solitude.
I am cold. I remember — it's hard to believe,
not even ten years have passed since —
the rare light days of euphoria.

Nobody ever gave a thought to Doom then,
not even in Berlin, which had outlived

its own end long ago. The island of Cuba
did not reel beneath our feet. It seemed to us
as if something were close at hand,
something for us to invent. We did not know
that the party had finished long ago,
and that all that was left was a matter
to be dealt with by the man from the World Bank
and the comrade from State Security,
exactly like back home and in any other place.

We had tried to get lost and to find something
on this tropical island, where the grass grew
over ancient Cadillac wrecks. The rum had gone,
the bananas had vanished, but we
were looking for something else —
hard to say what it really was —
but we could not find it
in this tiny New World
eagerly discussing sugar,
liberation, and a future abounding
in light bulbs, milk cows, brand-new machines.

Mulatto girls at the street corners
cradling their automatic rifles
smiled at me in Havana, at me
or at someone else, while I worked
and worked on *The Sinking of the Titanic*.
I couldn't sleep, the nights were hot;
I lived by the sea; I wasn't middle-aged,
I was not a kid, but I was younger
than now by ten years, and pale with zeal.

It must have happened in June, no,
it was in April, shortly before Easter,
we took a walk down the Rampa,
it was past midnight, Maria Alexandrovna
looked at me, her eyes shining with rage,

Heberto Padilla smoked a cigar,
he had not yet gone to prison, but who
remembers him now, a lost man,
a lost friend, Padilla, and a deserter
from Germany shaking with shapeless laughter,
he too went to prison, but that was later,
and now he is here again, back home, boozing
and doing research in the interest of the nation,
and it is odd that I still remember him.
There is not much that I have forgotten.

We talked and jabbered away in a medley
of Spanish, German and Russian
about the terrible sugar harvest
of the Ten Million Tons — nowadays
nobody mentions it anymore, of course.
Damn the sugar! I came here as a tourist!
the deserter howled, and then he quoted
Horkheimer — Horkheimer of all people,
in Havana! We spoke of Stalin, too,
and of Dante, I cannot imagine why,
cutting cane was not Dante's line.

And I looked out with an absent mind
over the quay at the Caribbean Sea,
and there I saw it, very much greater
and whiter than all things white, far away,
and I was the only one to see it out there
in the dark bay, the night was cloudless
and the sea black and smooth like mirror plate,
I saw the iceberg, looming high
and cold, like a cold fata morgana,
it drifted slowly, irrevocably,
white, nearer to me.

Notice of Loss

To lose your hair, to lose your temper,
if you see what I mean, your precious time,   ˙
to fight a losing battle,
losing height and luster, sorry,
never mind, to lose on points,
let me bloody well finish,
to lose blood, father and mother,
to lose your heart, lost long ago
in Heidelberg, all over again,
without batting an eye, the charm
of novelty, forget it, to lose
civic rights, I get the message,
to lose your head, by all means,
if it can't be helped,
to lose Paradise Lost, what next,
your job, the Prodigal Son,
to lose face, good riddance,
two World Wars, one molar,
seven pounds of overweight,
to lose, lose, and lose again, even
your illusions long ago lost,
so what, let us not waste another word
on love's labor lost, I should say not,
to lose sight of your lost sight,
your virginity, what a pity, your keys,
what a pity, to get lost in the crowd,
lost in thoughts, let me finish,
to lose your mind, your last penny,
no matter, I'll be through in a moment,
your lost causes, all sense of shame,
everything, blow by blow,
alas, even the thread of your story,
your driver's license, your soul.

FOURTH CANTO

Those were the times! I believed
in every word I wrote, and I wrote
The Sinking of the Titanic.
It was a good poem.
I remember exactly
the way it began, with a sound.
"A scraping sound," I wrote,
"stopping short. Silence." No,
it wasn't like that. "A thin jingling,"
"a clatter of silver." Yes,
that's the way I began, I think.
More or less. And so forth.
I quote from memory.
I forget the rest.

What a pleasant feeling it was
to be ingenuous! I didn't want to admit to myself
that the tropical party was all over.
(What do you mean by party? It was need,
you bloody fool, need and necessity.)
A few wretched years afterward,
now, it's all finished,
there are plenty of shoes,
plenty of light bulbs and unemployed,
brand-new machines and regulations.
I feel the cold in my bones,
an anachronism
within an anachronism.

I can smell the coke burning.
It is here I reside,
in the most hideous city of Europe,

amongst slowly rotting Prussian princes
and members of the Central Committee,
in bitter, anguished, national seediness,
and I remember, and recollect
my recollections. Don't worry,
I used to tell myself, it's just a fata morgana,
in actual fact the island of Cuba
does not reel under our feet.

And I was right then,
because at that time nothing foundered
except my poem
about the sinking of the *Titanic*.
It was a poem penciled
into a notebook, wrapped up
in black oilcloth, I had no copy,
because on the entire island of Cuba
there was not one sheet of carbon paper
to be found. Do you like it? I asked
Maria Alexandrovna, and then
I put it into a buff Manila envelope.
It was shipped from Havana harbor
in a mailbag for Paris
which never turned up again.

We all know the rest of the story.
Outside it is snowing. I try
to take up the thread, and sometimes,
now, for example, I think I have found it.
I pull. The veil is rent in two
with a hissing sound, and in the broad daylight
I recognize all of them:
the mulatto girls, the Captain
with his white whiskers, Dante
(1265–1321), Jerome, the stoker
(first name unknown) (1888?–1912),

the Old Master from Umbria
with his paint-stained fingernails,
born in such and such a year
and died thereafter,
Maria Alexandrovna (1943–   ) —

All of them, those
who froze to death, those who drowned,
1217 altogether, it is said, or 1500,
according to others. Go on squabbling,
maggots! Argue, deathwatch beetles,
about their numbers!
I for one know them all,
even the five Chinese, flattened
like flour bags against the planks
of the lifeboat. I think I know them,
I think they are still alive,
but I would not take an oath on it.

And so I am sitting here, wrapped up
in blankets, while outside the snow
is coming down. I am playing around
with the end, the end of the *Titanic*.
I've nothing better to do.
I have time, like a God.
I have nothing to lose. I deal
with the menu, the radiograms, the drowning men.
I collect them, I pick them up
from the black, icy waters of the past.

Debris, broken sentences,
empty fruit crates, heavy Manila bags,
buff-colored, soaked, soiled by the brine,
I fetch verses from the waves,
from the dark, warm waves

of the Caribbean,
teeming with sharks,
with dismembered verses, with life belts
and swirling souvenirs.

FIFTH CANTO

Take what they have taken from you,
take by force what has always been yours,
he shouted, freezing in his undersized jacket,
his hair streaming beneath the davits,
I am with you, he shouted,
what are you waiting for? Now
is the time, pull down the barriers,
throw the bastards overboard
with all their trunks, dogs, lackeys,
the women as well, and even the kids,
use brute force, use knives, use your bare hands.
And he showed them the knife,
he showed them his bare hands.

But the steerage passengers,
emigrants, all of them, stood there
in the dark, took off their caps
and listened in silence to what he said.

When do you want to take your revenge
if not now? Or do you mean to say
that you cannot bear to see blood?
What about the blood of your children,
what about your own? And he scratched his face
and cut his own hands
and showed them the blood.

But the steerage passengers
listened to him and did not move.
Not because he did not speak Lithuanian
(he didn't), nor because they were drunk
(they had long since emptied

their ancient bottles,
wrapped in coarse handkerchiefs),
nor because they were hungry
(though they had not eaten much):

It was something else. It was
hard to explain.
They understood quite well
what he said, but they did not
understand him. His words
were not their words. Worn
by other fears and by other hopes,
they just stood there patiently
with their carpetbags, their rosaries,
their rickety children
at the barriers, making room
for others, listening to him, respectfully,
and waiting until they drowned.

SIXTH CANTO

Unmoved, I look at this bare room in Germany,
at the high ceiling, which used to be white some years ago,
at the soot coming down in tiny flakes,
and while the city around me is darkening rapidly,
it is my pleasure to recover a text
that probably never existed. I fake my own work,
I restore my images. And I ask myself what the smoking lounge
looked like on board the *Titanic,* and whether the gaming tables
were checkered or covered with baize. What was it like
in actual fact? And in my poem? Was it in my poem
at all? And what about that thin,
absent-minded, excited man roaming Havana, involved
in disputes, metaphors, endless love affairs — was that me?
I'm not prepared to take an oath on it. And in ten years from now
I shall not be sure that these very words are my own,
written down where Europa is at its darkest, in Berlin,
ten years ago, that is, today, in order to take my mind
off the evening news and the endless succession of endless minutes
that sprawl before us the closer some sort of end seems to be.
Two degrees below zero, everything outside is black now,
even the snow. I am overcome by an enormous calm. I don't know why.
I gaze outside like a god. There is no iceberg in sight.

The Iceberg

The iceberg is drifting nearer,
irrevocably.

Look, it is breaking loose
from the glacier's face,
from the glacier's foot.
O yes, it is white,
it moves, O yes,
it is larger than anything
moving on the waters,
in the air,
or on the face of the earth.

Mortal dreams,
traversed by a caravan
of icebergs:
"Looming over the ocean,
more than two hundred and fifty feet high,
its surfaces, freshly fractured,
reflect the light
in hues and tints
of wonderful transparency."
"It is as if the sun's fire
were mirrored
in the windowpanes
of a hundred palaces."

It is better
not to think of the weight
of the iceberg.
He who has witnessed it,
will hardly ever forget

the sight of it, if he lives
for a long time to come.

"It is an exalting spectacle,
but it also inspires the heart
of the beholder
with a feeling
of secret dread."

For the iceberg
there is no future.
It floats on.
We have no use
for the iceberg.
It is indubitable.
There is no money in it.
Cosiness
is not its forte.
It dwarfs us.
We never see more of it
than the tip.

It is perishable.
It does not care.
It does not make progress,
but "when,
not unlike a monstrous
white marble slate
mottled with bluish veins,
it suddenly tilts and crashes down,
the ocean will tremble."

It is none of our business,
it will drift on in silence,
it needs nothing,
it has no offspring,

it melts away.
It leaves nothing behind.
It disappears to perfection.
Yes, that's the word for it:
perfection.

SEVENTH CANTO

We continue our guided tour and shall now see
the Palm Room, which is used as an intimate ballroom.
The magnificent paintings on the wall, especially
commissioned for the *Titanic,* are done in the Oriental Style.

> *Dinner   First Class*
> April 14, 1912
> Caviar Beluga
> Hors d'oeuvres variés
> Turtle Soup

The folding doors over there connect to the Turkish bath,
watch your step, where at all hours water cures and massages
under medical supervision may be obtained.
Please note the columns executed in red Carrara marble.

> Consommé Tapioca
> Lobster American Style
> Baked Salmon with Horseradish Sauce
> Curried Chicken
> Almond Rice   Tropical Fruit

The pair of bronze nymphs at the entrance of the Grand Foyer
are cast in the authentic Renaissance manner.
One represents Peace, the other Progress.
Ladies and gentlemen: dinner is now being served.

Last Supper. Venetian. Sixteenth Century

I

As soon as I had finished my *Last Supper,*
thirteen yards by five and a half,
a monstrous job, but rather well paid,
the usual questions came up:
What exactly do these foreigners mean
with their halberds? They are dressed
like Germans, or like heretics.
Do you think it is normal
to depict Saint Luke
with a toothpick in his hand?
Who put the idea into your head
to sit Moors, drunkards and clowns
at Our Lord's table?
Do we have to put up with a dog
sniffing around, a dwarf, a parrot
and a Mameluke bleeding from his nose?
My Lords, I said, all this
I have invented for my own pleasure.
But the seven judges of the Holy Inquisition,
in a flutter of red silk robes,
murmured: That's as may be.

II

Oh, I have done better than that
in other paintings,
but nobody else can do a sky
the color of this one;
and I am pleased by these cooks
with their long butcher's knives,
by these men clad in slashed hoods
trimmed with fur, in aigrets

adorned with heron feathers, in diadems
and pearl-studded turbans;
not to mention the muffled people
who have mounted the most distant rooftops
of my alabaster-faced palaces,
leaning over the parapets at a dizzy height.
What they are looking for
I cannot tell. But they do not even glance
at you, or at the saints.

III
I have told you again and again:
There is no art without pleasure.
This is true even of the endless Crucifixions,
Deluges and Massacres of the Innocent
which you ask me to execute —
I cannot imagine why.
So when the sighs of the critics,
the subtleties of the inquisitors
and the probings of the scribes
became too much for me,
I rechristened my *Last Supper*
and decided to call it
A Dinner at Mr Levi's.

IV
Just wait and see who will have the last word.
Take my *Saint Anne, the Virgin and Child,* for example.
Not a very amusing subject.
But underneath the throne,
on the checkered marble floor
done in sand-rose, black and malachite,
I put, as a redeeming grace,
a soup turtle with rolling eyes,
elegant feet and a shield
of translucent tortoiseshell.

A marvelous idea.
Like an enormous, perfectly arched shell comb,
the color of topaz, she glowed in the sun.

V
But as soon as I saw her crawling,
I thought of my enemies.
The gallerists babbling,
the academicians hissing,
and the belching of the prigs.
I took up my brush
and I buried my creature
beneath a few carefully done tiles
of black, green and rose-colored marble
before the parasites had a chance
to explain her to me.
Saint Anne is not my most famous work,
but perhaps my best.
No one except me knows why.

EIGHTH CANTO

Salt water on the tennis court can be quite a nuisance;
but then again, wet feet do not mean that the end of the world is at
     hand.
People are rather too eager for Doom to come,
like suicides looking for an alibi. This is likely to lead
to a failure of nerve and of reasonable discourse.
Nobody actually likes to drown, especially at two degrees below
     freezing.
If, at the moment of danger, the passengers' judgment
isn't as measured as one would hope —
fair enough! After all, I am sitting here myself, shuddering
on this godforsaken steamer, First Class, it is true,
and with a goblet of truly remarkable vintage port.

But let us assume for a moment that the *Titanic* is about to go down,
though I myself, being an engineer, and not much given to fantasy,
hold that this outcome is quite out of the question — so what?
We should not make too much of it. Statistically speaking, you see,
there are, at any given moment in time, a few dozen ships in distress
and nobody gives a damn, because they happen to be called
Rosalind II or *Land of Promise* instead of *Titanic*! And again:
Remember that there are thousands of boats afloat at this very
     moment
on the seven seas that will reach port punctually
and quite unaffected by our private disasters.

Furthermore, at the root of all innovation there is catastrophe:
new tools, new theories, new emotions — that's what we call
     evolution.
And thus, even if we imagine, just for the sake of argument,
that *all* ships were to go down on one and the same day, why,

in that case we should simply have to come up with something new —
enormous sky gliders, or trained whales, or iron clouds.
Or else lead stationary lives. The trees have been doing so for some
        time,
with obvious success. And in case we should be at a loss for ideas —
so much the worse for us. Other forms of life have died out, after all,
to our advantage, I should think. Where would we be now,
if the winged reptiles and the dinosaurs had not at some point
met with certain problems which proved too much
for their brains? Do you see what I mean?

From which I conclude that it does not make sense to consider
any old episode involving ourselves, for example our own demise,
from an all too narrow point of view. What I, as an engineer,
and inveterate port wine drinker, am saying, is, of course,
not entirely new, and this is why I am about to go under.

NINTH CANTO

All those foreigners who were posing for photographs
in the canefields of Oriente, their knives raised high,
their hair sticky, their cotton shirts stiffened
by sweat and syrup: superfluous people!
In the entrails of Havana, you see, the ancient misery
went on rotting regardless, the city smelled of old piss
and old servitude, the water taps ran dry in the afternoon,
the gas flame went out on the range, the walls
crumbled, there was no fresh milk, and at night
"The People" were queuing up patiently for a pizza.
But where the gangsters used to dine long ago, and senators
with blue-feathered striptease queens on their plump knees
used to haggle about their baksheesh, at the Nacional,
on the hotel terrace facing the sea, now just a few
forlorn old Trotskyites lingered, exiles from Paris,
feeling "sweetly subversive," tossing breadballs
at each other, and stale quotations from Engels and Freud.

> Cena   14 de abril 1969
> (Año del Guerrillero Heroico)
> Coctel de langostinos
> Consomé Tapioca
> Lomo a la parrilla
> Ensalada de berro
> Helados

Later on, in black and white, from the saloon a few gamblers
appeared on the promenade deck in evening dress,
ladies in pearl-studded robes, bystanders in dressing gowns,
idly picking up chunks of ice, in an old Hollywood movie.
It was close to midnight, the air was humid and hot.
The run-down cinema on the Calzada de San Miguel

was swarming with half-naked children giggling and climbing
over the dirty seats. The image was dim and grainy,
the soundtrack cackled: it was a rotten print.
On the snow-white deck planks Barbara Stanwyck
was hopping about with Clifton Webb, the frames danced,
and promptly, as always, chaos sprang from necessity.
Don't forget your revolver, dear, think of the sandwiches,
of your emeralds, of your manuscript. You take the Bible,
and you the little tin pig which plays "Maxixe"
whenever you twist its tail, your little piggy
of colored tin, don't leave it behind!

Delegations. Mulatto girls. Comandantes. In the dining room
the hungry poets from Paraguay are still carrying on
their feud with the Trotskyites in a cloud of cigar smoke.
On the fire escapes youthful police spies are hanging on,
softly humming their rhumbas, observing Czechs
who glance at their flashy watches and think of slimy deals.

First the noise, then the terror. The assaulted ear
cannot take it in. It is your feet that tell you:
the hull resounds, the roaring steam bursts from the funnels.
The furnaces are put out, the bulkheads come down,
the engines have stopped. It is still now, all of a sudden,
terribly still. A numb feeling, as if you had started up
from a nightmare, at four o'clock in the morning,
in your hotel room, listening. No sign of life.
Even the Frigidaire is silent. Now you would welcome any sound,
the heating pipes bonking, a burglar, a police raid . . .
Never again will it be as dry and as quiet as it is now.

Security Considerations

I am trying to lift the lid,
logically, the lid
on my private crate.
It isn't a coffin by any means,
it is just a package, a cabin, or,
in a word, a crate.

You know what I mean
when I say *crate,* come on,
don't play the fool,
all I mean
is an average crate,
just as dark as your own.

Of course I want to get out,
and therefore I knock,
I hammer against the lid,
I call out *More light,* I gasp,
logically, pounding away at the hatch.

So far so good. Unfortunately,
for security reasons,
my crate does not open,
my shoe box has a lid,
a rather heavy one to be sure,
for security reasons,
since we are dealing here
with a container, an Ark
of the Covenant, a safe.
There is no way out.

For our liberation, joint action
would, logically, be needed.

But for security reasons
I am all alone in my crate,
in my very own crate.

To every man his due! And hence,
for me to escape, by joint action,
from my own crate, logically
I would have to be out of it
to start with, and this condition obtains,
logically, for all of us.

Thus I break my very own back
against the lid. Now!
A chink, a narrow gap! Ah!
Marvelous! The open country
outside, covered with tins,
containers, or just plain crates,
in the background the high-rolling waves
ploughed by seaworthy trunks,
the enormously distant clouds above,
and lots and lots of fresh air!

Let me out, I proceed to cry,
feebly, with my tongue coated, against
my better judgment, covered with sweat.
To make the sign of the cross: impossible.
To beckon: no, I am short of hands.
To clench the fist: out of the question.

And hence I cry: *I express
my regrets, woe to me,
my very own regrets,*
while with a hollow *plop*
the lid, for security reasons,
comes down again
over my head.

TENTH CANTO

So this is the table at which they sat.
From the outside you see, through the porthole,
B. in the smoking lounge, an exile from Russia,
gesticulating, veiled in a blue haze
of exquisite smoke from Cuban cigars,
trademark Partagas, made by hand,
perfectly happy and oblivious of himself,
at the green table, not paying any attention
to icebergs, deluges, shipwrecks,
busily preaching the gospel of revolution
to a small band of barbers, gamblers
and telegraph operators. You see him,
but you cannot hear what he says.
The thick convex glass of the porthole,
reflecting the brass of the fittings,
is soundproof. Inaudible words — and yet
you know what he's driving at,
and that he is right, even if it is now too late
in the day to be right about anything.

Now, however, you notice, at the next table,
another gentleman, flushed with anger, rising
to his bait. He owns a Manchester mill, he finds
this nonsense revolting, he is indignant,
and scathingly he expounds
the advantages of iron discipline
and the blessings of strict authority.
Aboard a ship, he maintains, his mustache
trembling, just to give an example,
it has to be absolute and unwavering!
You, of course, cannot follow
his argument, since you do not hear it.

But just look at the way the gamblers
and the telegraph operators crane their necks,
as if a tennis match were going on!

By and large we would like to be rescued,
all of us, even you. But isn't this asking too much
from an idea? The match will end in a draw.
Nobody noticed these two gentlemen
in one of the lifeboats, nobody
has ever heard of them again.
Only their table is still around,
a bare table afloat in mid Atlantic.

The Reprieve

Watching the famous eruption of a volcano on Heimaey, Iceland,
which was broadcast live by any number of TV teams,
I saw an elderly man in braces showered by sulfur and brimstone,
ignoring the storm, the heat, the video cables, the ash
and the spectators (including myself, crouching on my carpet
in front of the livid screen), who held a garden hose,
slender but clearly visible, aimed at the roaring lava,
until neighbors joined him, soldiers, children, firemen,
pointing more and more hoses at the advancing fiery lava
and turning it into a towering wall, higher and higher,
of lava, hard, cold and wet, the color of ash, and thus postponing,
not forever perhaps, but for the time being at least,
the Decline of Western Civilization, which is why
the people of Heimaey, unless they have died since,
continue to dwell unmolested by cameras
in their dapper white wooden houses,
calmly watering in the afternoon
the lettuce in their gardens, which, thanks to the blackened soil,
has grown simply enormous, and for the time being at least,
fails to show any signs of impending disaster.

ELEVENTH CANTO

Let us out
We are suffocating
Our stockcar lurches
Our cupboard totters
Our coffin gurgles
We fight on the stairs
We pound against the panels
We break open the doors
Let us out
There are too many of us
Our numbers increase
the more we fight
for an inch of space
for a plank for a board
We are too close
to rid each other of lice
to nurse or to thrash each other
The pickpocket cannot lift
his crushed hand
nor the murderer his knife
We suffocate one another
Our imprisoned fury
flays our skins
and expires
Our numbers increase
horribly
We crush those
who have been trampled down
a soft mass
A panic pudding
reeking of fear

acidly ratlike
We go down softly
bloated and sagging
soggily

TWELFTH CANTO

From now on everything will proceed according to plan.
The iron hull does not throb anymore, the engines
lie still, the fires have been put out long ago.
What is the matter? Why don't we make headway? Listen!
Someone is murmuring in the gangway, telling his beads.
The sea is glassy, black, smooth. There is no moon.
Please do not worry. Nothing has gone to pieces yet,
not a vase, not a single champagne glass. People wait
in small groups, without a word, restless, obedient,
in their dressing gowns, fur coats and overalls.
Cables are being rolled up, awnings taken away
from the boats, davits swung out. The passengers
look slightly drugged. This fellow for instance
drags a cello along over the endless deck,
you can hear the spur scraping and scraping away
at the planks, and you begin to think:
I must be hallucinating — O look! A rocket is going up!
But then there is only a feeble hiss, a bluish flare
fizzling out in the sky, reflected in blank faces.
Liftboys, massage girls, bakers line up on the deck.
Aboard the *California,* a decrepit tramp, twelve miles away,
the wireless man in his bunk turns over and falls asleep.
Attention! Women and children first! — I wonder why.
Answer: We are prepared to go down like gentlemen.
I see. Sixteen hundred are left behind. An incredible calm
reigns aboard. This is the Captain speaking. It is now
two o'clock sharp, and I order: Every man for himself.
Now for the last tune the bandleader raises his baton.

THIRTEENTH CANTO

The ship is reeling in the gale,
eleven on the Beaufort scale . . .
       Nothing can uphold my goings,
       strength to conquer I have none . . .
              The sea is furious and mean,
              no star or moon is to be seen . . .
Hold me up in mighty waters,
let my weary soul abide . . .
       I often think:
       It's all over now,
       I am so alone . . .
              The day in night, declining,
              says I must, too, decline.
But then I get wise
and I realize:
It's no use to moan . . .
       E'en though it be a cross
       that raises me,
       still all my song would be:
              Well, a jolly old sailor
              with his arms akimbo
              is well prepared, is never scared,
              Rosemarie!
Though, like the wanderer,
the sun goes down,
darkness be over me,
my rest a stone . . .
       Doomsday isn't round the corner,
       just because I have the blues . . .
              Why wait, I say, and wither
              'mid scenes of death and sin?

I don't want to be a mourner,
I want my lover and my booze . . .
            I rise to glory, hither,
            and find true life again.
                        Why, everything looks pretty rotten,
                        and you think the end is near . . .
But even now, when hell is loose,
and your heart is filled with fear . . .
            yet in my dreams I'd be
            nearer, my God, to Thee . . .
                        For a jolly old sailor
                        is not bound for limbo,
                        he's never scared, he's always spared,
                        Rosemarie!
And happy angels o'er me
tempt sweetly to the sky . . .
            Doomsday isn't round the corner,
            for this world is still some use,
                    still it is
                        still it is
                            still it is
                                still it is
                                    still it is fit for use!

The above lines are adapted from the following hymns:
"Nearer, my God, to Thee" by Sarah Flower Adams (ca. 1840)
"Autumn" by H. F. Lyte (ca. 1910)
"Das kann doch einen Seemann nicht erschüttern" by Bruno Balz (1939)
"Davon geht die Welt nicht unter" by Bruno Balz (1942)

FOURTEENTH CANTO

It is not like a massacre, not like a bomb;
there is no blood, nobody's being mangled;
it is just a swelling, a steady increase,
all over the place. Dampness is seeping in.
Tiny pearls are forming, droplets, trickles.
What happens is that your soles are getting moist,
your cuffs are drenched, your collar is clammy
in the nape; your spectacles are fogged;
it is oozing from the safes, the plaster roses
on the ceiling are stained. What happens is

that its odorless smell pervades everything.
It drips, spouts, pours, gushes forth;
not one of these things at a time but all of them,
blindly, coincidentally, promiscuously,
wetting the biscuit, the felt hat, the drawers,
lapping sweatily at the wheelchair's tires,
stagnating brackishly in the urinals, leaking
into the ovens; then again it is just there,
horizontal, wet, dark, quiet, unmoving, simply rising,
slowly, slowly lifting small objects, toys, valuables,
bottles filled with disgusting fluids, carelessly
carrying them until they wash away,
rubbery things, dead, broken things; and this goes on

until you feel it yourself, within your breastbone,
the way it urgently, saltily, patiently interferes,
something cold and nonviolent coming up, touching first
the hollows of your knee, then your hips, your nipples,
your collarbones; until you are in it up to your neck,
until you drink it, until you feel the water

thirstily seeking your inside, your windpipe, your womb, your mouth; and you know what it wants to do: it wants to fill up everything, to swallow, and to be swallowed.

FIFTEENTH CANTO

After dinner, over the fruit, we asked him if he was not bothered
by the inky blackness of his metaphors, dripping with deepness.
Rather *passé,* we should have thought, all these hidden meanings.
Fashion, we were bound to observe, was implacable, and to this rule
Art was not an exception. Too much was too much. And Cuba,
why Cuba, of all places? What has Cuba to do with it? It must be
an *idée fixe.* What are you driving at, we asked, with your tall tales
about painting, about Gordon Pym, Bakunin and Dante?

It is you, he shouted, throwing about pieces of meat and bread,
who sink your forks into my slightest hints, messing up
meanings, rasping words, carving up what I have to say. It is none
of my doing, he went on angrily. I am bewildered, I stammer,
I mix and jumble, contaminate, jabber away, but I swear to you:
This ship is a ship! — he was now quite beside himself —
and the canvas being rent in two — he nearly chanted this bit —
symbolizes a canvas being rent in two, no more and no less,
do you get me? And let me tell you, I am like this canvas rag,
stretched to the breaking point. And he snatched the tablecloth
      from the board.

Gibberish, we retorted, high-strung nonsense. Mumbo jumbo!
But he sprang to his feet. I do not discuss, he said quietly,
I teach. Sprang to his feet and was on the point of leaving.
We had a mind to stab this creep in the back with our bread knives,
we were so angry. But at the door he turned back and started
all over again: You forget (in his most disdainful manner) —
I have eaten the flesh of man, just like you and like Gordon Pym!
I heard the rattle in the old anarchist's throat, next door,
on his soiled pillow, while I embraced his wife, smilingly.
By you, of all people, I will not be fooled. And besides
(he absolutely refused to go) — what could I do?

Do you think it is I who has cooked up this story
of the Sinking Ship which is a ship and yet is not?
The madman believing himself to be Dante is Dante.
There is always a passenger bearing this name on board.
Metaphors do not exist. You don't know what you are talking about.

Sheer confusion, we shouted, confusedly. This isn't a poem,
it's mumbo jumbo. He finally went away. He went,
and we looked at each other and looked at our fruit knives
and asked ourselves whether there can be metaphors
so sharply honed. Then we went on eating our pears and apricots.

SIXTEENTH CANTO

The sinking of the *Titanic* proceeds according to plan.
It is copyrighted.
It is 100% tax-deductible.
It is a lucky bag for poets.
It is further proof that the teachings of Vladimir I. Lenin are correct.
It will run next Sunday on Channel One as a spectator sport.
It is priceless.
It is inevitable.
It is better than nothing.
It closes down in July for holidays.
It is ecologically sound.
It shows the way to a better future.
It is Art.
It creates new jobs.
It is beginning to get on our nerves.
It has a solid working-class basis.
It arrives in the nick of time.
It works.
It is a breathtaking spectacle.
It ought to remind those in charge of their responsibility.
It isn't anymore what it used to be.

SEVENTEENTH CANTO

We are sinking without a sound. As if in a bathtub
the water is standing still in the brightly lit palm rooms,
tennis courts, lobbies, reflected by looking glasses.
Inky minutes pass by and congeal to dark jelly.
No disputes, no squabbles. Muted dialogues.
After you, sir. Give my love to the kids.
Don't catch a cold. In the boats you can hear the cables creak
and watch the phosphorescent drops from the sea, tossed up
in slow motion, dripping back from the blade of the oar into the sea.
Only when the end is at hand, and nobody asks the time,
when the last light in the hull has gone out,
when the dark bow has risen from the bottomless waters
and towers, absurd and perpendicular,
an unheard-of sound will smash the glassy calm:
"It was a rumble, or rather a roar, a smash, or rather
a succession of smashes, as if in an enormous vault
tons and tons of heavy things were hurled down the stairs from
      the top,
smashing each other and the stairs and everything in their way.
It was a noise no one had ever heard before,
and no one wishes to hear again in his lifetime."
From this moment on there was no more ship.
The next thing we heard were the cries.

Cold Comfort

Man's struggle against man,
according to reliable sources
close to the Home Office,
will be nationalized in due course,
down to the last bloodstain.
Kind regards from Thomas Hobbes.

A civil war fought with unequal arms:
one man's tax return
is another man's bicycle chain.
Poisoners and incendiaries
are planning to form a union
and call for job protection.

Our prison service
is utterly open-minded.
They offer Kropotkin's *System
of Mutual Aid in the Natural World,*
bound in washable black plastic covers,
as a study course. This is cold comfort.

We have learned to our dismay
that there is no justice,
and furthermore, to our even greater dismay,
from informed sources beaming with satisfaction,
that nothing remotely like it
can, should or will ever exist.

It is not yet quite clear
whose fault this may be. Original Sin?
Genetics? Methods of infant care?
The lack of polite education?

Capitalism? Unhealthy diet?
The Devil? Or Male Domination?

Unfortunately we cannot refrain
from rape and from ravishment,
from nailing each other down
to the nearest crosswalk
and from gobbling up the remains.
To find out why would be nice,
balm on the wounds of Reason.

We are annoyed but not surprised
by our daily atrocities.
What we find puzzling
are mild ministrations,
groundless generosity
and angelical sweetness.

It is therefore high time
to praise with fiery tongues
the waiter listening for hours on end
to the impotent man's lamentation;
the biscuit salesman showing mercy
and tearing up at the last moment
the writ of execution;

the bigoted spinster hiding,
strangely enough, the deserter
hammering breathlessly at her door;
and the kidnapper, suddenly tired
to death, giving up his tangled work
with a feeble, contented smile.

With a shrug we put the newspaper down,
filled with joy, the kind of joy
we feel when the B-picture

finally draws to an end, the lights
come on in the cinema, outside
the rain has stopped, and we long
for our first puff of smoke.

EIGHTEENTH CANTO

Whereupon, the white voice said, they rowed
as fast as they could, away
from the blank, impervious spot
where the *Titanic* has disappeared,
but they did not escape the cries.
Each of these voices was clear and different
from the next, the shrill scream of fear
different from the hoarse roar,
the imploring yell from the choking howl,
and so on, the voice went on evenly,
and so forth, and there were not a few
crying voices, but a thousand of them,
and the sea was calm, mind you, a lull
was in the air, the voices, the voice said,
carried quite far, they were very distinct,
and thus in the boat some said, let's turn back,
we have room to spare, by no means,
they would crowd the boat and capsize it,
said some others, and drown us all in an uproar,
and thus they went on quarreling and rowing, until
after a very long hour's time, the voice said
flatly, the voices diminished, and only here
and there a solitary, feeble cough
was to be heard, a barely audible animal squeak,
foundering simply and soon in the dark.

Because the moment
when the word *happy*
is pronounced
never is the moment of happiness.
Because the thirsty man
does not give mouth to his thirst.
Because *proletariat* is a word
which will not pass the lips of the proletariat.
Because he who despairs
does not feel like saying:
"I am desperate."
Because orgasm and *orgasm*
are worlds apart.
Because the dying man,
far from proclaiming:
"I die," only utters
a faint rattle,
which we fail to comprehend.
Because it is the living
who batter the ears of the dead
with their atrocities.
Because words come always
too late or too soon.
Because it is someone else,
always someone else,
who does the talking,
and because he
who is being talked about,
keeps his silence.

NINETEENTH CANTO

There was a man in the sea, floating
on a plank, on a wooden board, on a table,
no, it wasn't a table, it was a door,
which he hung on to, rolling
and lurching, he felt something icy
flooding his face every now and then,
but it did not devour him. He saw nothing,
nobody saw his eyes, he kept his small face
pressed against the plank, a small man,
spread-eagled, as if a larger hand
had nailed him to the door.
Only dead men seem so small. Some
passing by in a boat called out to him,
but he did not answer. He must be dead,
a few of them said, but others wanted to help.
The old quarrel all over again. They rowed
past him, they quarreled, they turned back.
They pulled him on board and unfastened the knots
by which he had crucified himself
to the latch and the hinges. It is a child!
some said, turning him over, and started
to rub his hands. But it was a Japanese.
He opened his eyes, he spoke in his native tongue,
and not many minutes had passed
before he sprang to his feet, raising his arms,
jumping, stamping his feet, and forthwith
he seized the oars and rowed until dawn,
stroke upon stroke, chattering happily
all the time. He was not dead,
he was not the Messiah,
and nobody understood what he said.

The Tripoli War. Conflicts in German Social Democracy. Seventh International Congress on Tuberculosis. Outrageous Behavior of Dortmund Workers on Strike.
New York 24-hour lending rate 3 3/8. New York sight bills on Berlin 95 1/8. London light crude 39/3 cash.
Paris. According to a bulletin issued by the aeronauts, the balloon *Fantasque* has been driven out to sea, caught by a hurricane.
Berlin. In a motion to support the Armament Bill it is argued that the transition from peacetime to a state of war must be facilitated. Comparative statistical tables have been published in order to clarify how the increased effective force of the army will affect conscripts of different age groups.
Wanted, assiduous person wishing to become self-employed and to make a speedy career. No capital or previous experience needed.
Shipping News. Arrivals: S.S. *York* at Naples, S.S. *Zieten* at Bremerhaven, S.S. *Queen Louise* at Antwerp, S.S. *Bülow* at Aden, S.S. *King Albert* at Genoa, S.S. *Princess Alice* at Colombo, S.S. *Germanicus* at Havana, S.S. *Prince Eitel Friedrich* at Hamburg.
Tucked in our warm beds we hardly notice when our earthbound fellow creatures are shivering outside, when vicious April frosts kill without mercy the delicate tissue of prematurely flowering buds. From our Gardening Correspondent R. Schwerdtfeger (Munich).
Berlin. We learn from reliable colonial sources that H.H. the Duke of Mecklenburg will definitely be appointed Governor General of Togo. Dr Schnee will succeed the Viscount Rechenberg in German East Africa.
The Stage. Augsburg: *Chaste Susanna*. Basle: *Pillars of the Community*. Bremen: *The Waltz Dream*. Düsseldorf: *A Doll's House*. Frankfurt: *Dashing Fellows*. Freiburg: *The Chocolate Girl*. Cologne: *Europe Makes Merry*.
Berlin. Today's stock exchange opened firmly. Great attention was paid to New York trends and to the news from the Upper Silesian iron market in sheets and bars.

Munich. For the time being, the relations between Bavaria and the Reich are said to be satisfactory.

Paris. The representatives of the Six Power Committee have decided to cancel the monthly advance payments granted to the Chinese government.

Wiesbaden. The plumbers' and electricians' strike ended today after two weeks. The journeymen have been awarded an increase of 1 1/2 cents per working hour.

Weather Forecast from the Meteorological Service of the Frankfurt Physical Society. An extensive high pressure area has established itself over Central Europe; therefore, fair weather and rising temperatures are to be expected for tomorrow.

Deutsche Bank 255.50, Daimler-Benz Motors 244.00, Siemens & Halske 241.90, AEG 262.00, Höchster Farbw., 575.00

Are you anemic? Use Patermann's Bath Cubes regularly for lovely rosy cheeks.

Frankfurt. The German Trade Counselor in Calcutta draws attention to the excellent export opportunities for motorcars in British India.

New York. Today's early Reuter cables confirm the fact that all passengers of the *Titanic* have boarded the lifeboats safely and in calm waters.

TWENTIETH CANTO

The eighth of May was one hell of a day,
when the *Titanic* was sinking away.
Captain was in his quarters one lonely night,
black man called Shine was off on the port side.
Shine was downstairs eating his peas,
till the goddamn water come up to his knees.
Shine went up on deck, said, "Captain, I was eating my peas,
till the goddamn water came up to my knees."
Captain said, "Shine, Shine, sit your black ass down,
I got ninety-nine pumps to pump the water down."
Shine went downstairs, looking through space,
till the goddamn water came up to his waist.
Shine went up on deck, said, "Captain, I was looking through space,
till the goddamn water came up to my waist."
Captain said, "Shine, Shine, sit your black ass down,
I got ninety-nine pumps to pump the water down."
Shine went downstairs, eating his bread,
till the goddamn water came up to his head.
Shine went up on deck, said, "Captain, I was eating my bread,
till the goddamn water came up to my head."
Captain said, "Shine, Shine, sit your black ass down,
I got ninety-nine pumps to pump the water down."
Shine said, "There was a time, your word might be true,
but this is one goddamn time your word just won't do."
Shine took off his shirt, he jumped and took a stroke,
was off in a minute like a motorboat.
Captain said, "Shine, Shine, save poor me,
I'll give you more money than any black man see."
Shine said, "There's money on land, and there's money on the sea.
Take off your shirt and take a dive like me."
That's when the Captain's daughter came up on the deck
with her hands on her pussy and drawers round her neck.

She said, "Shine, Shine, save poor me,
give you more pussy than any black man see."
Shine said, "There's pussy on land and there's pussy on the sea,
but the pussy on land is the pussy for me."
Shine went on and on, quite like an eel,
kept on stroking, and met up with a whale.
The whale said, "Shine, Shine, you swim mighty fine,
but if you miss one stroke, your black ass is mine."
Shine said, "You may be king of the ocean, king of the sea,
but you gotta be a swimming motherfucker to outswim me."
When the word got to Washington that the great *Titanic* had sunk,
Shine was on the corner, damn near drunk.

Adapted, by permission, from Roger D. Abrahams, *Deep Down in the Jungle: Negro Narrative Folklore from the Streets of Philadelphia* (Chicago: Aldine Publishing Company, 1970).

TWENTY-FIRST CANTO

Afterward, of course, everybody had seen it coming
except we who have perished. Afterward
premonitions were rife, and rumors, and scenarios.
All of a sudden dog races were mentioned, dog races
held on C-deck, a highly irregular sport to indulge in
aboard a ship; brightly painted iron hares,
moved by an ingenious contraption, were purported
to have induced mottled greyhounds to illicit exertions;
and many a destitute passenger is said to have lost
his last guinea at this dreary pastime; not to mention
the ship's bell showing cracks; the claret
at the launching, Château Larose '88, gone sour;
the mysterious behavior of the rats at Queenstown,
the last port of call; and the hushed-up case
of the verger running amok in the ship's chapel.
Ominous incidents, unspeakable vices: granted, but why
should we bear the blame? How could we suspect
that there were dowagers getting themselves whipped
under the card table by depraved cabin boys,
that girls under age were appealing for help
through the air duct, and that in the Turkish bath
hermaphrodites were showing their orifices? Now,
by hindsight, everybody claims to have heard the organ
playing, untouched by any human hand, all night long
unholy tunes, as a last warning to whom it might concern.
"Divine Nemesis" — easily said, after it happened!
The penultimate words of a portly gentleman for example,
naively addressed to another portly gentleman
shortly before putting out to sea: Not even God himself
could sink this ship! Well, we haven't heard them. We
are dead. We had no idea. We did not feel it in our bones.

Keeping Cool

Sometimes, not very frequently, hunting hares in the winter,
you will perceive in the snow, or shortly before Easter,
peering through the half-open window of your sleeping car,
against the dawning day, on the roof of a lonely barn,
on a pile of coal, or on a belvedere across the valley,
a small flock of people dressed in black coats,
led by a prophet with steel-rimmed spectacles
and flared nostrils, motionless, silent, waiting
for Doom to come. We, of course, go on bothering
about our humdrum business, supposing the deluge
to be something antediluvian, or else
an elaborate practical joke — while they, perched
on their respective lookouts, know exactly the moment
When. They have returned their hired cars in good time,
emptied their Frigidaires and prepared their souls.
Terribly thin is the sound of their voices,
swept by the wind across the freeway, the shady dell
due for development: "Nearer, my God, to Thee."
In the long run, however, it can hardly be helped
that first one, then another will glance at his watch
and be taken aback; the prophet's arm, raised in admonition,
will go to sleep; and while the weak sun rises,
the train passes by, the coal is burnt up,
the snow melts away and the hares end up in the oven,
first one, then another will slowly come down
and join us in the nether regions of routine,
meeting the mockery of the commonplace,
buying a toothbrush, reopening his bank account
and bracing himself for the inevitable holidays.
Even the prophet himself, faced with the small print
and with dirty linen, will have to make allowances,
hanging on, however, to the essentials.

His voice may crack but it does not fail him.
Outward appearances do not matter. What are weeks
or even centuries, compared to Eternity?
He for his part will not be surprised
by the Day of Reckoning. I told you so, he will mutter.
Things just couldn't go on like this. But unfortunately
nobody listened to me. And thus even now he feels,
perched on the top of his barn and crowing away,
that Doom, however unpunctual, will always be
a tranquilizer of sorts, a sweet consolation
for dull prospects, loss of hair, and wet feet.

TWENTY-SECOND CANTO

Far away in the gulf, out there in velvety darkness,
I saw the fumbling searchlights of a destroyer.
It was snowing inside my head. The old Havana
gasped for breath, going down the drain shamelessly.
The nights were soft. It was the time when I used to roam
the cinemas in the suburbs, the crowded posadas,
the ancient Mafia bars with their empty counters.
I heard lovers rustle in the dead underbrush
behind the walls of the cemetery. Instead
of writing about the sugar harvest and Socialism
on One Island, like a good comrade,
I fished the dead and the survivors, who had died
long since, from the black waters, impartially
and half a century after the fact. I looked
into their eyes, and I recognized them all:
Gordon Pym, Jerome the stoker, who never uttered a word,
Miss Taussig, Guggenheim (copper and tin),
Engels (textile), Ilmari Alhomaki, Dante —
I was cold and afraid, but I recognized them
by their fingernails, secrets, hats, desires —
I distinguished their shrieks of terror
in the tropical dark, in the moonlight I saw
what they clasped in their numbed fists:
wax roses, cast-iron keys, blank sheets of paper.
With my back to the future I studied
statistics and floor plans, and they all confirmed
what I knew: We are in the same boat, all of us.
But he who is poor is the first to drown.

	First Class	Second Class	Steerage	Crew	Total
Embarked	325	285	1316	885	2201
Saved	203	118	499	212	711
Lost	122	167	817	673	1490

In the beginning there was only a small sound,
a scraping sound easy enough to describe.
But where it would lead to I did not know.
Imperceptibly Berlin was buried in snow, in isolation.
Softly the sea lapped at the Malecón, oily and nowhere.

Model toward a Theory of Cognition

Here is a box for you,
a large box
labeled
Box.
Open it,
and you will find
a box in it,
labeled
Box from a box
labeled Box.
Look into it
(I mean this box now,
not the other one),
and you will find a box
labeled
And so on,
and if you go on
like this,
you will find,
after infinite efforts,
an infinitely small
box
with a label
so tiny
that the lettering,
as it were,
dissolves
before your eyes.
It is a box
existing only
in your imagination.
A perfectly empty
box.

TWENTY-THIRD CANTO

Contradictions! he shouted, discrepancies! doubts!
The number of casualties, for example: 1635?
1715? or 1490? He had elbowed his way to the front,
seized the microphone and asked his question:
Ladies and gentlemen, dear listeners,
where shall we put our faith? He was a poet
with plenty of muscle, he pushed
the others aside who were poets as well,
more or less, and he shouted: O empirical fact!
I'm going out of my mind! O eternal discord
of experts! Woe betide the counsel's opinion!
O bibliographers, I pity you, you will go under,
and nobody will look you up again, ever,
and you will sink without glory, amen! — Nonsense,
another one howled from the pack. Believe me,
he shouted and snatched at his colleague's cable
until he let go of the mike: They believed
what they read in the papers, afterward,
all of them, even the witnesses and the victims
did not believe their own eyes, and we agree
with them and say: It must have been like a movie.
Now a few very hefty poets came up arm in arm
and held the stage, a poets' collective,
turning their elbows out and chanting in unison:
Welcome, rumors, welcome, legends
and even lies, the wilder the better. Silence
down there in the audience. Let us have some applause
for Edward J. Smith, our white-bearded Captain,
who, after thirty-eight years of blameless service,
corrupted by greedy shipowners, eager to make
a record run, goes full speed straight at the iceberg,
and now he shrieks: Be British, before he puts

the barrel of his revolver into his mouth.
Bravo! For after all, what kind of poet is he
who will not swallow the salty soup
and lick the dripping slops from the boiler shell?
Verily verily I say unto you: unless you feel
in your very bones the cold sweat of panic,
the clammy drizzle of history, you had better shut up.
Three cheers for the Countess Rothes in her nightgown,
witch, suffragette, depraved lesbian,
gaining full sway over lifeboat and crew
and proclaiming the rule of women! Cheers
for the officers tumbling down the gangways,
blind drunk, and emptying their guns at the rabble
from steerage: Wogs, Jews, camel drivers and Polacks —
we must teach them a lesson!
A band of black-faced stokers is routed
and driven back down again into the engine room
where the inky water is knee-deep now,
while all the time, less than four miles away
Captain Lord is leaning idly over the breastrail
of his rotten tramp, with all engines stopped
and the wireless operator turned in for the night,
so the Captain is free to enjoy the distress signals
and the drowning cries, untroubled by messengers.
Cheers, my dear friends! There is always someone around
just looking, impassively forming a balanced opinion,
with the notorious twitching at the corner of his mouth.
By now the poets were raving, shouting demands, confessions:
a pack beyond any control. Stop him! they shouted,
stop the veiled millionaire disguised as a woman,
with a magnificent turban on his head, who enters
the last lifeboat before the ship goes to pieces!
"Nearer, my God, to Whom" plays the band, no,
"Ragtime," "One last cigarette, and all is done and said," no,
"Lord of Mercy and Compassion," nothing of the sort
is being played, there is no band left,

there was not a sound, not a word to be heard,
there was nobody left to raise three cheers,
three cheers, ladies and gentlemen, for you,
for the poets, for all of us.

This is not Dante.
This is a photograph of Dante.
This is a film showing an actor who pretends to be Dante.
This is a film with Dante in the role of Dante.
This is a man who dreams of Dante.
This is a man called Dante who is not Dante.
This is a man who apes Dante.
This is a man who passes himself off as Dante.
This is a man who dreams that he is Dante.
This is a man who is the very spit image of Dante.
This is a wax figure of Dante.
This is a changeling, a double, an identical twin.
This is a man who believes he is Dante.
This is a man everybody, except Dante, believes to be Dante.
This is a man everybody believes to be Dante, only he himself
    does not fall for it.
This is a man nobody believes to be Dante, except Dante.
This is Dante.

TWENTY-FOURTH CANTO

On the second day of the voyage the morning watch
found tents on the promenade deck. Where do they come from?
Who has put them up? What are these people doing here?
Light olive faces, dark ochre complexions.
Some even say that they were daubed like savages.
Sailors with boarding axes drove them away,
but overnight, more and more numerous, they returned.
A smell of mutton came from the hatchways,
white smoke from charcoal fires, ash
all over the place. Women appeared, bedecked
with spiraling bracelets of gold, in garish rags,
little mirrors on their breasts. Naked urchins
were climbing barriers, parapets, railings. Old men
in wide trousers and large turbans sat silently
around their hookahs behind the wireless room,
wearing sabers, or rather silver daggers
and scimitars. On the sun deck, between the boats,
veiled ladies were to be seen taking the air,
all in white, and burnoosed gentlemen. And then,
suddenly, the cymbals rang. What do you mean?
Cymbals, I said. Right there in mid Atlantic,
not far from the Great Newfoundland Banks, there were cymbals.

The purser was at a loss to explain
these remarkable sights. But I am here to tell you,
cried Salomon P., the drawing-room artist, I know!
I recognize them! These are the nomads I painted,
they have sprung from the walls of the Palm Room.
The image has come alive. I drink too much.
You can see that my hand is trembling. But the nomads
come after me: My image, they cry, is my self! Never again
am I going to paint. Do not turn around, ladies

and gentlemen! I am afraid of their knives.
Yes, John Jacob Astor said, I can see them, too.
By now they were swarming all over the ship,
lighting torches. Their shouts were incomprehensible.
They had their camels with them, their swaying shadows
obscuring the brilliance of the brass fittings.
And then, on the morning of April fourteenth,
they had all at once vanished, leaving nothing behind
but a desert smell and the dung of their cattle.

The Rape of Suleika. Dutch, late 19th Century

A small man, crooked and grizzled, with a glass in his hand,
he leans, shortly before Easter, on the iron railing
in front of his house on Prinsengracht,
turning his back on the street, as if it were an ocean.
There is a breath of gin wafting
over the small, crooked, grizzled steps.
He drinks rather more than is good for a painter's hand;
and between two sips, looking past her
and cracking jokes about his age, Salomon Pollock
tells a young Muslim girl
whose half-veiled eyes he cannot do without
all about his painting, of which, drunk
or not drunk, he never loses sight for a moment.

To the left, he says, you will see *The Rape of Suleika.*
Here, behind the high wall, in the garden,
under palms and mimosa trees, by the fountain,
where enormous lilies pour forth their scent, white,
innocent, intoxicating, lascivious (it is unbelievable
how tall these flowers have grown) — here, my beauty,
the sultan's daughter reclines, adorned with pearls
and with dates, the trappings of lust and magnificence.
The dark hand of a eunuch holding a fan
makes for a breeze. Until at long last
the bearer, covered with dust, steps forward
and discovers himself as a prince
by his talisman made of leek-green jasper
and by the tamed falcon attending him.

The Old Masters — believe me, there is no such thing.
I ought to know. For thirty years now
I have been a preserver of all good things:
half an alchemist and half a joiner.

I was unsurpassed as a restorer,
detailing for the world at large, punctiliously
and with the utmost care, by means of resin,
wax and saliva, Lost Paradises,
Virgins, Shipwrecks, Last Judgments,
Persian as well as Flemish and Florentine,
recovering things that never existed
with my lancet, my sponge and my spatula:
a faithful forger, whose daily bread
was the past, a past of my own doing,
the apple of my eye, the best we can hope for.
It is there for all to see, at the Rijksmuseum,
a fraud, sublime and moving, a wonder
of the world, and a pious patchwork.

Next comes my centerpiece: *The Bedouins' Feast.*
A desert night, glittering with lances
and shotguns and with the flashy tinsel
of belly dancers, their golden earrings
jingling, and the drums and the cymbals rumbling.
The horseman on the dapple-gray steed
in the glare of the torches is the emir's son.
The woman he holds, his prey, half-naked,
half-draped in zinc-white glazed muslin.
Her teeth, they say, shimmer like hailstones,
her lips are redder than carnelians,
she smells of aloe, of ambra, of nard
and of cinnamon. That's what they say.
The horses are neighing, and amid the shouts
of the warriors the wedding is consummated.

Blindfold I saw, through layers of paint,
feeling the varnish, the wood of the frames,
scraping at the cracks of the canvas
with my X-ray fingers: I was infallible.
When you finally see it, the exhibit,
cleansed, newborn, botched, resplendent

— after I have rubbed it down, puttied and fixed it,
my angel, with these very hands — you will find
a tiny square left untouched in a corner,
showing off the filth of the centuries,
the muddle, the ever imperfect remorse
of posterity, which is beyond redemption.
I used to spend hours and hours
pondering this dark remnant,
which exposes me and my manipulations.

And finally, to the right, there is *Vengeance*.
Behold the long shadows the horsemen cast
in the early light, and the grand vizier's pavilion
standing out against the battlements of the city.
It is strewn with paillettes sparkling in the sun.
Behold the vultures gliding high in the thin air,
the muskrats in the thicket, and the camels
ruminating serenely at the wayside.
Behold the henchman swathed in a black turban,
as he sheaths his sword, and over there
the severed head on the palisade. You see?
Don't you see the sultan in his sedan chair?
How distraught he is, as he opens
without misgivings, smilingly,
the poisoned book?

And thus I abandoned the art of dissimulation
and resolved to paint "myself." Do you know
what it means to paint on your own? Sometimes
I don't know "myself." I am second-rate.
My hand trembles. It is not the gin.
It is not fame. It is history
with its unending sham and duplicity.
I am her invention, and she is mine.
An eternal tug of war. Quite so.
I, Salomon Pollock, decorating the walls

with an Orient made up of hot air,
a drawing-room artist. Yes, my odalisque.
Now I hope you realize how eloquent are my lies.
The truth, a dark window down there
in the corner, the truth is mute.

TWENTY-FIFTH CANTO

The last boat, Collapsible C, Engelhardt type,
loaded and lowered on the starboard side,
exact time: one forty-seven,
crew: six men.

Quartermaster G. T. Rowe
(in charge), Pearce
(pantryman), Weikman
(barber) and three firemen.
Passengers: Gordon Pym (ghost),
J. B. Ismay, Esq. K.B.E., F.R.G.S.,
shipowner of S.S. *Titanic,*
President, White Star Line
of America, Inc., coward,
eyes like glass marbles,
pomade-greased hair.
The rest: women and children.
Total load: 35,
disorders and incidents: none.

Only at dawn,
when the icebergs lit up
rose-colored against the horizon,
only when, in the face of salvation,
"the sun's fire seemed to be mirrored
in the windowpanes
of a hundred palaces,"
a bundle of limp rags
came to life under the feet
of the thirty-five seafarers.
Something began to move,
something wrapped up in dirty canvas,

dripping and tattered,
awoke and began to speak.
Five strangers came to light,
five Chinese stowaways.

To this very day nobody knows
how they had come aboard the *Titanic,*
nameless, penniless, without papers,
not speaking a word of English,
how and when they had settled down in the boat,
and what has become of them.

O prophets with your backs turned to the sea,
with your backs turned to the present, O sorcerers
looking placidly into the future,
O shaman priests forever leaning over the railing —
one single paperback leafed through
is enough to see through your mysteries!

Reading in bones, in stars, in debris,
from entrails, all that has been and all
that is bound to happen, for the public good,
O Science! be blessed and blessed be
the rather minor rays of light which you offer us,
half bluff and half statistics: mortalities,
money supply targets, increasing entropy . . .

Go on! All these brimstone-colored illuminations
are better than nothing at all,
they keep us happy on sultry summer nights:
computer print-outs fresh from the backroom,
sample probes, excavations, tip-offs
based on the Delphi method — hear, hear!

Blessed be your interim reports!
For the time being there is enough fresh water left,
the skin is still breathing expectantly,
my skin twitches, our skin, and even yours,
you dead-alive medicine men,
notwithstanding the question of tenure,
the footnotes and the likelihood of advancement —
for the time being the end (an interminable,
finely scattered Act of God)
is not yet final — a comforting thought!

And hence, my dear accessories before the fact,
while off Newfoundland icebergs are being forecast
and thunderstorms in the sulfur-lined skies
of Central Europe, you had better get out
of your institutes for the weekend. Run
for your life, or a slice of it, an interim,
whatever that may mean, until Monday;
though as a basis for your predictions
this course of action may not be much good.

O my friends, ever thirsting for knowledge,
I pity you, resting at your dachas,
your Irish cottages, or in Korčula,
turning your backs on the sea
and switching your brains off, placidly.
Onward, and may your torch never go out
during the Ping-Pong match! I bless you.

TWENTY-SIXTH CANTO

178. Exterior. Open sea.
Sunrise.
The scene is a replica of Scott's famous painting
in the London Academy.
Wide, blue expanse of ocean (miniature).
Very long shot.
A ring of crystal icebergs
in brilliant colors.
Behind them the sun rises.
Music.
Medium shot.
The sea, seen from an iceberg.
Back projection.
In the distance a small fleet
of lifeboats (models).
Camera zooming in slowly.
Narrator's voice:
The fifteenth of April, 1912,
was a gorgeous spring day.
Cut. Camera at sea level. Medium shot.
A lifeboat with passengers.
Upward pan.
Narrator's voice:
The first sea gulls
from the Grand Banks have arrived!
Messengers of salvation,
of life!
Music swells (violins).
Fade out.
Lettering on the darkening screen:
THE END.

TWENTY-SEVENTH CANTO

"In actual fact nothing has happened."
There was no such a thing as the sinking of the *Titanic*.
It was just a movie, an omen, a hallucination.
"In actual fact" they go on playing their game of whist,
and if it isn't whist, it's backgammon; the cigar boxes
in the smoking lounge are still handmade in Cuba,
radiant with gold medals; Peace and Progress
hover forever over the entrance to the Grand Foyer,
costive allegories with hard bronze bosoms;
the rich have remained rich, and the Comandantes
Comandantes; in the Turkish bath Mrs Maud Slocombe,
the world's first ship's masseuse, is doing her duty,
still going strong. Chandeliers all over the place,
velvet draperies, palms and looking glasses,
Louis XV, Louis XVI: it's enough to make anybody sick.
Of course, nowadays we offer a Christmas bonus to the crew
and color TV in the cabins; the steward is from Jamaica;
the nurse has a degree in psychology; but otherwise
nothing has changed. The menus are still too large.
On F-deck, it is true, there is now a Finnish sauna,
where the Central Committee is sweating, taking their tea
with saccharin instead of sugar; the glaciologists
have brought their microcomputer along for the worldwide
symposium on climate research, printing out on-line
iceberg simulations for the next hundred and fifty years.
The boutiques are doing a roaring trade, as usual,
in *Titanic* ashtrays and *Titanic* T-shirts,
in the cinema *A Night to Remember* is showing,
and the happy end is routine, just like the holdups,
the panel discussions about pension funds,
about Medicare and Socialism on One Steamer.

Every now and then there is a wildcat strike
with the waiter duly dropping the champagne cooler
and the pianist stopping short in the midst of the Fantasia in C minor.
The gangsters and the publishers are taken aback,
the chic artists are not amused, the military attachés
ask for the bill; it is all great fun and excitement.
The only one to have second thoughts is a judicious whore
who thinks: "This is the way the world will end,
to the cheers of witty men who think it is all a joke."
The poets, too, are still hanging around
at the Café Astor, helping themselves
to Cuba libres from plastic cups.
They look slightly seasick and remember dutifully
the steerage passengers, the Chicanos, Eskimos
and Palestinians. The phony poet nods
to the middling poet; the middling poet
winks at the real thing; then each of them
retreats to his cabin, leaning back in his dry easy chair
and writing, as if nothing had happened, on the dry sheet:
"In actual fact nothing has happened."

Dept. of Philosophy

No doubt we are intelligent. But far
from changing the face of the world, on stage
we keep producing rabbits from our brains
and snow-white pigeons, swarms of pigeons
who invariably shit on the books.
You don't have to be Hegel to catch on to the fact
that Reason is both reasonable and against Reason.
All it takes is a look into your pocket mirror.
You will see yourself wearing a blue gown,
spangled with silver stars, and a pointed hood.
For the Hegel Congress we meet in the cellar
where our card-file colleagues are buried,
unpack our crystal balls and our horoscopes,
and go to work, waving our expertise,
our pendulum and our research reports.
We make the tables turn, we ask reality
How real is it? Hegel is smiling,
filled with *schadenfreude*. We daub his face
with an inky mustache. He now looks like Stalin.
The congress is having a ball, but there is
no volcano in sight to dance on. The guards
outside are on their guard. Our psyche
calmly produces pertinent statements,
and we agree that deep down in any given brutal pig
a well-meaning public servant is to be found,
and the other way round. Abracadabra!
Like an enormous handkerchief we unfold
our theories. The plainclothes men
in their trench coats are modestly waiting
in front of the riot-proof seminar shelter.
They smoke, they hardly ever make use of their guns,
they keep guard on our faculty roster, our paper flowers
and the snow-white pigeon droppings all over the place.

TWENTY-EIGHTH CANTO

Peering through the porthole on the sixth floor of the hotel
I watch the Asians with their pregnant wives camping
in the hall of Kazanskaya Station, covered in blankets,
on the platforms of Haydarpasa Central, the icy sleet
pounding the panes, I hear the ship's bell sounding,
all Havana I see at my feet, sparkling in the tropical night,
the unemployed are pushing their way out of the crowded lifts,
milling about in the bluish emergency light of the passageway,
before my watering eyes pressed to the spy hole everything blurs,
the Norwegian, delirious because he has eaten shoe polish,
crouched by the rudder controls, is babbling away
and dissolves, my eyes are inflamed, vaguely I see
the Arabs out there in their bivouac, looking for women,
unshaven, starting a fire with old newspapers, drowned in smoke,
at the end of the long, long, worn-out, dirty coconut matting
where the last stragglers from some faraway revolution squat,
surrounded by hustlers and hotel dicks, eating with their bare hands
raw joints of donkey meat, I cough, the smoke makes my eyes water,
I totter, I hear music in my flooded head, I hear
a mad violinist telephoning the Captain, Land! he shouts,
land in sight! the end of the world! ice in sight, sugar, snow, heroin,
and I, shivering with fatigue and with damp, standing next to the fireax
under the night-light, by the extinguisher in the hotel staircase,
six floors above the Caribbean, and I would like to know
who are these gentlemen wearing medals, beards, syringes,
all these killers who throw their hats through the door on my bed,
solitude, I chant, solitude, filth and solitude, I cough,
all these people, nomads, drunks, fade and blur, going down
before my eyes, with me, after me, and dissolve, all of them,
and within my forty-six thousand gross register ton head
I can hear their voices calling each other for help on the telephone.

What were we talking about? Ah yes, the end!
There was a time when we still believed in it
(What do you mean by "we"?), as if anything
ever were to founder for good, to vanish
without a shadow,
to be abolished once and for all,
without leaving the usual traces,
the famous Relics from the Past —

a curious kind of confidence!
We believed in some sort of end then
(What do you mean by "then"? 1912? 1917? '45? '68?)
and hence in some sort of beginning.
By now we have come to realize
that the dinner is going on.

> Roast Turkey, Cranberry Sauce
> Boiled Rice
> Prime Roast Beef
> Baked Potatoes with Cream
> Watercress Salad
> Champagne Jelly   Coconut Sandwich
> Viennese Ice Cake
> Assorted Nuts   Fresh Fruit
> Cheese   Biscuits
> Coffee

Not even the eight hundred crates of shelled walnuts,
the five grand pianos, the thirty cases
of rackets and gold clubs for Mr Spaulding,
last seen at 42 degrees 3 minutes North
and 49 degrees 9 minutes West,

have been lost for all times:
here, before our eyes, they are bobbing up again
(What do you mean by "here"?), 65 years after the fact —

Bottled messages, and no end to the end!
All our love, scribbled down
on a cardboard box before drowning,
menus fished from the high seas,
picture postcards, the paper soaked,
the ink blurred with wine, with tears, with brine,
signs of life, hard to decipher, hard to get rid of —

Not to mention the Final Reports
of the competent Courts of Inquiry,
the expert opinions, pamphlets and memoirs,
and the Transactions of the Royal Commission,
twenty-five thousand pages
read by no one —

Relics, souvenirs for the disaster freaks,
food for collectors lurking at auctions
and sniffing out attics.
That April night's menu
has been reprinted in full facsimile,
and every month there is a new issue
of the *Titanic Commutator,* Official Organ
of the Society for the Investigation of Catastrophe —

Plans to lift the wreck by means of divers,
by gas balloons or by submarines,
The Original *Titanic* Model Set,
plastic, washable, one yard long,
copyright Entex Industries, Inc.,
$29.80 postpaid, a money order,
from Edward Kamuda, 285 Oak Street, Indian Orchard, Mass.
Full return privileges guaranteed!

True, the reproduction of a lifeboat
does not save anybody, the difference
between a life jacket and the word *life jacket*
makes the difference between survival and death —

But the dinner is going on regardless,
the text is going on, the sea gulls
follow the ship to the very end.
Let us stop counting on the end! After all,
we take no account of the fact
that our days are counted.

Something always remains —
bottles, planks, deck chairs, crutches,
splintered mastheads —
debris left behind,
a vortex of words,
cantos, lies, relics —
breakage, all of it,
dancing and tumbling
after us on the water.

The Rest on the Flight. Flemish, *1521*

I see the child playing in the corn,
who does not see the bear.
I see the bear hugging or killing a peasant.
He sees the peasant,
but not the knife
sticking in his back,
that is, in the back of the bear.

On the hill over there lie the remains
of a man who was put to the wheel;
but the minstrel passing by
does not notice them.
As for the two legions
advancing upon each other
on the brightly lit plain,
the flash of their lances is blinding me,
but they fail to observe the hawk circling overhead
who keeps a cold eye on them.

I distinguish the threads of mold
dangling from the roof beam
in the foreground, and in the distance
I perceive the courier galloping by.
He must have emerged from a ravine.
Never shall I come to know
what this ravine looks like from within;
but I imagine that it is damp,
very damp, and full of shadows.

To the center of the picture the swans
in the pond ignore me.
I see the temple on the edge of the precipice,

the black elephant on guard
(how strange to see a black elephant in the open fields!)
and the statues, who out of their white eyes
watch the fowler in the forest,
the ferryman, and the conflagration.
How silently all these things come to pass!

On very remote, lofty towers
with uncommon embrasures
I see the owls twinkling. O yes,
all these things I can well see,
but how should I know what matters
and what does not? How should I guess?
Everything here seems evident,
equally distinct, necessary
and impenetrable.

Out of my depth, lost in my own concerns,
just like the faraway city over there,
and like those other cities, even bluer
and even more distant,
dissolving into other visions,
other clouds, legions and monsters,
I go on living. I go away.
I have seen all this, but I cannot see
the knife sticking in my back.

THIRTIETH CANTO

We are still alive, one of us said,
sitting in the twilight:
We know better.

After these words
there was a silence.

In the most distant corner of the room
somebody coughed. It was winter,
it was Central Europe,
it was one of those afternoons
when the survivors slowly, cautiously,
begin to realize
that they are survivors,
when they turn up
in the deserted railway stations, in bunkers,
in tabernacles and other places.

Suitcases tied with string,
full of heavy souvenirs, were being opened.
Someone found a few abandoned tin cups,
a few dirty diapers, a few matches,
remnants of ship's biscuit
wrapped up in cloth, crumbs of tobacco.
Outside there was still
a faint light in the sky.

Strangely enough, the better part
of all that existed before
had disappeared, without leaving a trace,
like a stone in the water.

A damp smell, as if someone
had been ironing sheets,
was spreading over the room.
It was the pale breath of a girl
who stood with her back to the window,
taking away the last trace of daylight.

Now that the helicopters have disappeared
and nothing is smoldering anymore
or howling, now that the worst is over
and we do not care anymore,
we can begin from scratch.

Protestations in foreign tongues,
muddle, mumbling, a hum in the air.

First of all we must disinfect,
put in splints, mend, and dig graves.
Then we can think of revenge,
and after revenge, of repetition.

The stove was smoking. On the large table
in the middle of the room
something was spread out, perhaps
a heap of coats rolled up
or a bundle of awnings, sandbags
or bales of Manila paper.

Nobody even glanced at it.

For years we have been playing around
with the afflictions
that were in store.
Residual risk, we used to say,
leak, we called it, fail-safe threshold.
Christ, we said. Those were the days!

Two needles were then exchanged
for a small cake of soap.
A bony cat sniffed at the plaster
trickling from a crack in the wall.
Bandages were being changed.

One of the deserters
had swollen glands
and in the eyes behind his thick glasses
there was a whitish shimmer
as if he were drowned.

Everything we ever did was wrong.
And therefore everything was wrong
that we thought. I was there!
Don't try to console me, ever!
I can bear witness. Here,
look at my scars if you doubt it.
The scars are my proof.
And he showed us his arm,
gnawed at by unknown teeth.

In front of the door
a large pool of water had spread
and anyone coming in
left a wet trace behind him.

After all we might have done better
to fight. Yes, but when?
And how? What do you mean,
in good time? Was there ever
a good time? We had no choice.
Now we are poor, and there is calm.

They had shouted each other down.
They looked at each other. One,

wearing a turban, turned away from us,
shrugging. The stoker,
in his weary voice, had the last word.

Outside it started to snow heavily.
The age-old parquet floor
had cracked long ago.
Around our shoes
small puddles began to form.
An old man wearing a sable coat
began to pray tenderly.

A pound of Périgord truffles
rinsed in cold water, brushed,
peeled with great care,
cut in slices not thicker
than the blade of a knife,
bathed in clear butter
and tossed over the fire,
to be served with a sauté
of pheasant's breast —
I fail to remember the sauce.

With a wink we let him drone on.
Someone finally said: All right.
Let us get started.

Nobody moved.
There was a sound to be heard, perhaps
from the stove, a shrill, seething whirr,
piercing the darkened room.

THIRTY-FIRST CANTO

The Berlin Room was filling
with smoke, with survivors.
More and more of them, muffled
and out of breath, hammered
at the doors or pushed the windows open,
jumped in, shook the snow
out of their hair
and settled down
around the hissing stove.

The stoker raised his carbide lamp
and showed us the markings
of past floods on the wall,
dark lines, knee-high,
waist-high, brow-high,
in the hissing light.

The worst is over now!
Clamor, whispers, sighs
of joy and of anguish.
There is no end to the worst!
Avant nous le déluge!
Hold fast, for God's sake!
There was a burst of chanting,
a milling around,
a wading confusion,
a speaking with other tongues.
The room was reeling.
The survivors raved on
untiringly about their survivals,
until they got tired of it.

Then for a time nothing happened.
Nobody put on the light,
though it was very dark by now.
The snow outside the window
piled up higher and higher. This night
was not going to come to an easy end.

The bouncer brought some tea
in a pail. There was even some sugar left.
A stillness hung
over the blind corners of the room,
which seemed to age rapidly.

Some sat in a circle, on mailbags,
recited phrases
which they knew by heart,
and talked about a dead man.

It's just as well that he's dead.
Now we, the bereaved,
his foes and his women,
can finally cut out
from these notorious cantos
whatever we do not like.

We can cut him down to size.
Without us he is nothing.
It is our voices which come forth
from his dead hide,
and we can do with him
whatever we like.

Do you remember the way he sat around
naked, the way he wailed, the way he claimed,
waving his arms, that he couldn't go on,
that the thread was broken?

He was no good, he was like a corpse
fished out of the sea,
we could not care less
about his shrieks. They would not die down,
though the bathtub had long since run over.

Spendthrift, pedant, mystery monger!
Old beast of prey! Cold-blooded niggard
and renegade! True, there was a time
when we fed this mighty charlatan,
when we coddled him, warmed him,
pandered to his whims and desires —
but we hated his greedy saurian heart,
his leathery skin smelling of yeast,
of mold and of ooze —

In the meandering room
filled with the murmur
of widows, of women, of foes,
there was an indistinct form
spread out on the table, darkly,
like an enormous loaf.

Every now and then, as in a waiting room,
someone came or went, without so much as a nod.

Excuse me, I, for example,
am here to say, once for all,
that he was just a fraud,
that he had never been to Havana,
and besides, there are no icebergs in Cuba.
The whole thing is a hoax,
cribbed from old Sunday papers.

Nobody knew the speaker. He was
a small, podgy fellow wearing a hat,

92

by name of K., or something like it,
who used to be in the biscuit trade,
selling whole shiploads
of crispies and crackers.

The old bouncer who was shuffling around,
listening to us, stopped short,
stuck his thumbs in his worn,
red, gold-braided dolman
and announced solemnly:
A hundred years' forbearance
for the thief who steals from a thief!

All right, all right! Some of us laughed,
though we were not in the mood for jokes.
Forbearance? Never! The real Simon Pure,
sanctimonious as ever, rolling his eyes,
eagerly took his cue.
I am the real poet! I!
(He of all people! That total flop!)
I am the real Simon Pure, and I warn you!

He bogged down in a hotchpotch
of envy, jealousy, *angst*.
You could tell that he would die early
from his mother-of-pearl-colored fixer's eyes.
He got stuck in his speech, he choked,
the stoker slapped him on the back.

A woman appeared in an old-fashioned dress,
a Russian, or so it seemed by her name.
She wept. One of us gave her a hand
and helped her to step over the plank
in front of the door. Underfoot
the muddy water was gurgling.

She was very young, she was the shrewdest
of all the widows, and her eyes
glistened like wet cherries.

No, I am not mistaken.
He was a fossil, a flabby,
whining monster
looking like one of those whales
which used to be shown for money,
at country fairs, in a tent
reeking of antiseptic and putrefaction.
I loved him. I was dead set against him.
I told him that he was dead and gone.
Dead men tell no tales.

Now that we have our peace,
what are we going to do?
Isn't it nice and pleasant
to sit here by the shallow water?
No. Would it be better to leave?
No. To go on like this?
Not on your life.

The deserter who from the very beginning
had wanted us to stop his mouth
was groaning in his sleep.
The woman who was his foe
and the woman who was his friend
embraced, and washed, and rested.
The cat was still there.

Some were seasick. Others wept
and made love in the dark.
Sometimes we ate. Many grew weary.
We held fast.

Friend or foe,
it was all the same now.
Nobody asked the time.

It was a beautiful night,
the like of which only the tropics can offer.
We rested in our deck chairs
and closed our eyes.
The water was washing softly
against our ankles.

We were left over,
we went on breathing.
We had ended up here by chance.
We were all in the same boat.

THIRTY-SECOND CANTO

Later on, when the immense room
had darkened completely,
there was nobody left
except the dead man
and an unknown woman.

Foe and friend
had become one and the same,
something Other.

The unknown woman heard his even breath,
stooped down to him in the dark,
closed his mouth, kissed him,
and with her one and only mouth
took him along.

THIRTY-THIRD CANTO

Soaked to the skin I peer through the drizzle, and I perceive
my fellow beings clutching wet trunks, leaning against the wind.
Dimly I see their livid faces, blurred by the slanting rain.
I don't think it is Second Sight. It must be the weather.
They are right on the brink. I warn them. I cry, for instance,
       Watch out!
There's the brink! You are treading slippery ground, ladies and
       gentlemen!
But they just give me a feeble smile, and gallantly they retort:
       Same to you!
I ask myself, is it just a matter of a few dozen passengers,
or do I watch the whole human race over there, haphazardly
hanging on to some run-down cruise liner, fit for the scrapyard
and headed for self-destruction? I cannot be sure. I am dripping wet
and I listen. It is hard to say who the seafarers over there
may be, each of them clutching a suitcase,
a leek-green talisman, a dinosaur, or a laurel wreath.

I hear their feeble laughs, and I shout at them unintelligible words.
The unknown man covering his head with sodden newspapers
is presumably K., an itinerant biscuit salesman;
I've no idea who the man with the beard is; the one with the maulstick
is a painter called Salomon P.; the lady who sneezes incessantly
must be Marilyn Monroe, while the gentleman clad in white,
holding a manuscript wrapped in black oilcloth, is undoubtedly
       Dante.
These people are filled to the brim with hope and with criminal
       energy.
In the downpour they keep their dinosaurs on the leash,
they open their suitcases and lock them again,
chanting in unison: "The world will end on May thirteen /
We die / and that is awfully mean." Hard to say

who is laughing here, who pays attention to me and who doesn't
in this steam bath around me, and how close we are to the brink.

I can see my fellow beings going down very gradually, and I call out
to them and explain: I can see you going down very gradually.
There is no reply. On distant charter cruises there are orchestras
playing feebly but gallantly. I deplore all this very much, I do not like
the way they all die, soaked to the skin, in the drizzle, it is
a pity, I am severely tempted to wail. "The Doomsday year," I wail,
"is not yet clear / so let's have / so let's have / another beer."

But where have the dinosaurs gone? And where do all these sodden
      trunks
come from, thousands and thousands of them drifting by,
utterly empty and abandoned to the waves? I wail and I swim.
Business, I wail, as usual, everything lurching, everything
under control, everything O.K., my fellow beings probably drowned
in the drizzle, a pity, never mind, I bewail them, so what?
Dimly, hard to say why, I continue to wail, and to swim.

Havana 1969–
Berlin 1977